The Untold
KOREAN STORY

by
BOB PIERCE
as told to
KEN ANDERSON

ZONDERVAN PUBLISHING HOUSE
Grand Rapids, Michigan

CONTENTS

1. The Call 5
2. The Korean Church 9
3. Korean Christians 12
4. Martyrs for the Faith 16
5. Sights Along the Way 20
6. A Trip by Korean Railroad 26
7. The Gospel Preached 29
8. The Gospel Received 32
9. Pusan 35
10. Seoul 38
11. A Modern Exodus 45
12. Supreme Love for the Lost 50
13. Taejon 53
14. Kaesong 56
15. A Korean Saint of God 60
16. A Korean Bible Conference 65
17. Inchon 68
18. A Modern Joshua 71
16. And the Rain Did Not Fall 75
20. A Return Visit to Korea 78
21. Deliverance 84
22. Taegu and Farewell 87

CHAPTER ONE

The Call

It took G. I. blood to inform most Americans—including a good many evangelical Christians—that the peninsular nation of Korea is one of great significance in the confused pattern of present-day world history. The heroic stand along the Pusan beachhead, General MacArthur's brilliant surprise attack at Inchon, the drive to the Yalu, the counter-thrust of Chinese "volunteers"—these are now military history. The strategies, the success and failure are subjects for discussion from top Pentagon brass to lowly corner drugstore sergeants in the U.S.A. And across the world, it is the same.

The Korea story, in so short a time, has been told everywhere.

Yet there is another Korea story. Overlooked by the secular press, unnoticed by the great rank and file of mid-century Christendom, it has already been chronicled in heaven as one of the most significant spiritual eras since the book of Acts.

In fact, it is safe to say that—incredible as it may seem—the mighty working of the Holy Spirit in the lives of men made it necessary for the North Koreans to thrust their vicious attack below the 38th Parallel.

Syngman Rhee, gracious president of the U.N.-sponsored South Korean republic, personally told me that the reason Communism had been unable to destroy his government through termite tactics was because of the tremendous surge of spiritual passion which had come to his people.

As in China, so in Korea, the Communists tried to infiltrate South Korean thought at its fountain head— the schools. Because there was enough salt of the Gospel among the thousands of students, the endeavor failed. If it failed in the schools, Communism could not hope to succeed elsewhere.

I know of no greater tribute to the cause of missions.

Don't misunderstand me. I do not say Korea is a Christian nation. Cross section the rank and file of her people anywhere, and you will find idolatry, immorality and all that keeps company with these two agents of hell. But I can say that God is at work in Korea, that the impact of His Word is unmistakably evident wherever the Gospel has been proclaimed, and that consequently the impact of historic Christianity figures prominently in the unabridged story of what has actually transpired.

Like most Christians, I would have been pretty much unaware of this fact had it not been that the Lord strangely directed my path toward Korea—there to give me the greatest soul-winning opportunity I have ever known.

I had last been in the Orient back in 1948, and while there had held youth meetings in Pieping, residing at the Oriental Missionary Society of which Eddie and Ernie Kilbourne are members. They, when the political collapse came in China, did not return to the United States but, instead, went to Korea where their mission operates several schools.

During this and a previous trip to the Orient, my heart had been heavily burdened for Japan. However, since military restrictions made it necessary to limit activity, it had not been feasible to plan anything on a large scale there. But by 1950 General MacArthur had sent out his pleas for Christian workers of all kinds to challenge Japanese young people with the claims of

Christ. So it seemed that here was my opportunity to satisfy the deep heart longing I had for a ministry in this portion of the eastern harvest fields.

My heart thrilled at the thought of big meetings in Japan.

However, in the course of my planning, I dropped a note to my friends, the Kilbournes, in Seoul, asking them if they could arrange for me a week or two of meetings in Korea.

Unknown to me, that letter dove-tailed into God's plan for my own life in a most unusual way, for I immediately received a reply from the Kilbournes telling me that a great hunger for God had come to Korea. The Korean church was a living, spiritual, deep-rooted organism. Pastors and churches throughout the South Korean Republic had been praying for revival. There had been a national day of prayer asking God to deliver them from the threat of enemy forces dammed up behind the 38th parallel. During that day of prayer, thousands of people had turned out in one of the big stadiums in Seoul.

Now a nation-wide evangelistic campaign was being planned. Entitled "Save the Nation Evangelistic Crusade," it was to be a series of city-wide evangelistic campaigns in key cities throughout the Republic.

They had been concerned about a speaker, and wondered if I would come for a few weeks in that capacity.

Working on the committee were such godly men as Harold Voelkel, a member of the Presbyterian mission, and Otto De Camp, along with others whom I knew to be genuinely consecrated people.

This letter caused a strange stirring to come into my heart. After much prayer, I told them I would come for a month. So I left the plans completely in their hands, not knowing whether the meetings would be large or small.

The committee made one suggestion.. They wanted me to bring Gil Dodds, since Koreans are a sports-loving people with a special interest in running. Gill also agreed to come for a month.

Just before leaving America, God arranged another providential appointment. I went to the home of one of my friends for an evening of fellowship. Among those who had dropped in was Bob Findley, another outstanding athlete who had been a national inter-collegiate boxing champion at the University of Virginia. Bob was only in Los Angeles for a few hours this one night, as he too was on his way to the Orient—looking forward to a ministry among students in Japan.

We got to talking, and he said, "I hear you're going to Korea."

"Yes," I answered, adding in the same breath, "why don't you come along with me?"

"When are you going?" he asked. Then, before giving me a chance to answer, he said, "A year ago when I was in the Orient, I told the Lord that this coming April I wanted to be in Korea. All year long it has been on my heart. For some reason I have kept planning on that month. I don't know why."

I was struck to silence by this strange occurrence. Finally I told him that I, too, would be in Korea during the month of April.

And so it was that God led him to become the third member of our evangelistic party.

It was like the seal of God's approval. It gave me renewed confidence that the weeks which lay ahead would be weeks of divine appointment.

CHAPTER TWO

The Korean Church

I did not realize until we reached Korea that God had so definitely sent Bob Findley to join in the work. Because of the late hour, his name did not appear on the posters. We had little chance to publicize him among the Korean students.

This mattered little, however, for God seemed to have given him a special anointing of the Holy Spirit. In the days of our thrilling ministry there, he had the joy of leading almost ten thousand students in high school and universities to a public confession of Christ as Saviour during the nine weeks we worked together in Korea.

When we arrived, we found that all over Korea the leading sports writers, government officials, the Bishop of the Methodist church, the Presbyter of the entire Presbyterian Church and missionaries of the key churches in all Korea keenly anticipated the campaigns which lay before us. The missionaries had done a wonderful job preparing the entire South Korean Republic for our coming.

Beyond the publicity, important as it was, lay the greatest preparation of all—the preparations that God had made. I learned of it during our first campaign in the city of Seoul.

Speaking to one of the native pastors, a leader in the plans there, I suggested that we ought to have a prayer meeting each morning, asking God's blessing upon the efforts to be extended.

He looked at me rather strangely, and for a moment I wondered if he understood or if, perhaps, he did not take well to the idea.

Then, with a faint smile upon his lips, he said, "Which prayer meeting would you like to go to?"

I didn't understand.

"You see," he explained, "there is a prayer meeting in each of the churches every morning at daybreak. These prayer meetings have continued daily without interruption for the past five years, ever since our liberation from the Japanese."

I was just beginning to learn what a potent force for God the church in Korea really is.

That church was born in revival. Unlike so many of the churches in Japan, it was not educated into Christianity but was born through a spiritual awakening. From the very beginning men and women became Christians because they had an experience with God which gave them righteousness, consecration, separated living—an experience reflecting itself in an unusual measure of spiritual strength and endurance.

It took this kind of genesis to carry the Korean church through the years, because the Korean church has been a suffering church throughout the generations of its existence.

For the past fifty years Korea as a nation had been subjugated under the heel of Japanese imperialism. For the church, however, this was a blessing in disguise. People had few liberties, few outlets for their own individualism. Consequently, many turned to God.

Perhaps they couldn't make their voices heard in community and governmental affairs as they might have liked, but they could make their voices heard to God. The Korean church became a praying church.

Some of the missionaries explained the phenomena of the tremendous crowds attending early morning prayer meetings by saying that this was the Korean's outlet to voice the cry of his own soul—to give expression to the anguish and the suffering, as well as the frustration bound up within.

Whether or not that is true, I do not know. I do know that attending those prayer meetings was an indelible experience. These people pray with fervency, with a faith that reaches out and believes God from the moment of a prayer's utterance.

There is yet another interesting sidelight to these early morning prayer meetings. It is the fact that, like most Orientals, Koreans live in crowded quarters—a whole family customarily living in one or two rooms. These rooms must serve as living room, dining room, kitchen, bedroom, workshop, playroom and sickroom. In view of the fact that rarely has an entire family been Christian, it is a natural thing for a person who does not have the sympathy of all his family not to want to pray or try to have his devotions in the full hearing and view of folks who are unsympathetic.

So it is that these believers have formed the habit of getting together in these early morning prayer meetings, in order to find a sympathetic group with which to pour out their hearts to God.

These desires, however, do not adequately explain to me the reason for these morning prayer meetings. Similar conditions in other countries have not produced such spiritual fervor.

I do know that they are people who hunger after God. Of the some six hundred thousand professed believers in South Korea, a remarkable majority maintain a robust Christian testimony. No wonder Syngman Rhee saw in them a bulwark against atheism. No wonder God could take the simple preaching of the Word, given out by native pastors and missionaries and teams like our own, and bring in an abundant daily harvest of souls.

CHAPTER THREE

Korean Christians

The spiritual grain of these Korean Christians shows itself best in the depth of their consecration. Christianity is no mere veneer to these people. They walk with God, a walk which strikes a distinct departure from worldliness of any kind.

In most of the churches in Korea, the custom has long been established not to baptize a person, or take him into the church, immediately upon his conversion, but rather to wait several months until he has had a chance to prove himself.

During that time of probation, he must be faithful in attendance at the services of the church. His life must give evidence of the fact that he has become a new creature in Christ. Then, after he has walked circumspectly in the view of the Christian community, he is permitted to join the church.

This is significant. It means that when you say there are six hundred thousand church members in Korea, there actually are that many people who are faithful in their attendance at church. Not merely so many names on a group of church rolls, these people practice Christianity.

Another fact which keeps many superficial confessions of Christ from swelling the church rolls is the custom many congregations have of not permitting a new convert to be baptized or taken into the church until he has learned to read well enough to feed his own soul upon the Word of God. I met many older people who had

had to wait until they learned to read before they could be taken into membership.

At the outset, this may sound a bit harsh. But I know that in the Presbyterian church throughout Korea, for example, this has proved a wonderful thing. It has caused some people, who otherwise might have been careless and indifferent, to become avid students of the Word of God. When one realizes how cemented an Oriental becomes in his ways, as the years go by, this takes on increased significance.

Other price tags may be reckoned with in this matter of separation. Some of the greatest battles of Christian patience take place completely behind the scenes.

Like other Orientals, the Korean dreads alienation from his family, for his roots go down deep into filial piety. As a child, he is taught to revere and respect his ancestors. But since Christianity cuts a complete opposite to Buddhism and Shintoism, it often becomes necessary for new Christians to face intense persecution at home. It is no easy thing for a young Christian suddenly to break with tradition and refuse to participate with his family in pagan worship.

Christian girls face another problem. Girls are given in marriage as infants or young children, and practically the only security a young girl has for the future is the fact that a husband has been chosen for her. Korea has many girls who, having become Christians, are disowned both by their own families and by the families of their future husbands. Readjustment in such circumstances is not so simple as it would be for a girl in an Occidental community.

Then, too, separation for the new Christian includes an entirely new approach to morality. Koreans, as is true of many Orientals, have a lax moral standard. One of the country's greatest sins has been the sin of adultery and lasciviousness.

Consequently, one of the first things the church looks for is to see what stand the new convert takes in regard to his daily moral living. Because the Korean church has taken such a clean and clear stand on this issue, its members have maintained a high standard of conduct.

We were in Presbyterian churches, for example, where immorality was such an issue that if one of the members fell into sin, confessed and repented, five years had to pass from the time of his reinstatement before he could hold any position in the church. During those five years he was given loving counsel, but at the same time he was carefully watched to make sure his repentance had been genuine.

Most of the churches take a decisive stand against drinking and the use of tobacco. In one of the largest churches in Seoul we met a wealthy doctor who owns his own hospital. He had been one of the heaviest contributors, and came every morning to the prayer meeting before going to his hospital. In addition he stopped at the church every night on his way home for another half hour of meditation and prayer. Yet for seventeen years this doctor was not permitted to serve as an elder in the church—the church to which he was the largest contributor—because he owned a building in Seoul which he had leased to a number of business firms. One of these firms, unknown to him, had subleased a portion of the building to a tobacco merchant.

When his name came up for eldership in the church, it was decided that he could not have the position because tobacco was sold on property belonging to him.

The doctor tried to get this client to leave the building, but the man would not go, for it was an excellent location. The doctor offered to pay him to get out, but without success. For seventeen years he waited. Each year at the annual meeting of the church, his name was proposed for elder. Each year he was turned down because he had not been able to rid his property of the tobacco salesman.

Finally, in desperation, he sold his entire property in order to have his hands clean in the eyes of the church, and to be free of this merchant who had gotten into his building and who, by Oriental tradition, could not be driven out.

Such procedures may border on the fantastic to non-Christians, and even to many Christians in America, but this is Christianity in Korea. This is the standard set for a company of believers to whom godliness is not a side issue but a career.

CHAPTER FOUR

Martyrs for the Faith

The recent war in Korea, with all the heartache it
has brought to the people of the land, is but another
chapter in the book of suffering Christians have under-
gone. For the Korean church is made of martyr stuff.

When the Japanese thrust their military might upon
the people, Christians were ordered—by a governmental
edict under the guise of patriotism—to observe certain
Shinto ceremonies. Schools, for example, were required
to have shrines, and to begin each day with pledges of
allegiance to the emperor.

For Christian students this immediately called for
compromise or separation. Many refused to compromise,
and suffered greatly because of it.

Churches, too, were ordered to observe a certain
amount of Shinto worship.

The Japanese church, shot through with modernism
and higher criticism, could go along with the militarists. As a result, pastors escaped persecution by play-
ing into the hands of the militarists.

Not so in Korea. The more the Japanese threatened
Christians, the stronger became their faith. Hundreds
of pastors and Christian leaders went to concentration
camps rather than bow even in token obeisance to an
emperor who said he was God. They remembered
that God had said, "I the Lord thy God am a jealous
God. Thou shalt have no other gods before me."

We, of course, met many Christians bearing scars of
suffering inflicted by the Japanese. I think particularly

16

of Pastor Park, who assisted us in a number of our meetings.

He was picked up by the Japanese Thought Police, because of his influence in a number of the high schools where he had advised students not to bow to the Shinto shrine and thus compromise their Christian testimony.

Found guilty, the Japanese sent him to Manchuria. Bewildered, he thought of his banishment as an escape, a way out of the problems which arose from serving God in Korea.

Shortly after his arrival, a great flood engulfed the major portion of that area of Manchuria. During the course of the flood, he found himself trapped one day with a sudden rise of water, and forced to climb a tree to spare his own life.

For three days and three nights he remained in that tree, while water swirled angrily about him. Hungry, cold, dazed from lack of sleep, he got to thinking. There in that tree he determined that if God saved his life he would not take an easy way out. He would return to Korea, even though the Japanese had banished him, and help plead the cause of Christ among his people—even though it cost him his life.

Cautiously, he slipped back through the bordering mountains of North Korea, and returned to his city, his parish and his people.

Uncompromisingly, he began to herald forth once more the claims of the Gospel. As a result, a short time later he was picked up together with a group of other Korean pastors and imprisoned. The imprisonment, lasting for several years, involved torture and suffering. Many of the pastors died within a few months after the incarceration, unable to endure being packed into a stuffy little room with absolutely no sanitation and only the poorest and vilest kind of food.

Pastor Parks learned what it was to be taken out night after night, winter and summer, to a place called the "punishing grounds," sometimes forced to crawl at the prod of Japanese bayonets from his cell to the torture area.

Thirty-three times he received the water treatment. The tormentors would stuff a filthy rag into his mouth, and then—having strapped him to a table—pour a bucket of water down through his nostrils. With his arms and legs held immobile, he had no way of dodging or turning.

He remembers being tortured to the point of unconsciousness on eleven occasions. The last two times, he was given what they call the Japanese soup treatment— liquid, heated and with pepper added, forced down his nostrils.

On another occasion, in the dead of winter, enemy soldiers forced him to strip naked. Then, while he stood in the snow, buckets of cold water were thrown over him until frost bit his hands and feet so severely that to this day he has neither fingernails or toenails.

On several other occasions, he suffered a punishment that renders a man almost incapable of moving his arms or legs. His hands were tied behind his back; then, by means of a rope tied to his hands, he was suspended from the ceiling just high enough so that his feet did not touch the floor.

As if this were not enough, they also tied both his hands and his feet—so that he could not protect himself—and then rolled him over and over on a concrete runway, beating his nose and his cheeks to a bloody pulp.

Finally, after three years and six months of this treatment, Pastor Park's mind broke. His oppressors, deciding that he could no longer give them any particular enjoyment, released him.

For two long years he roamed the streets, until Christian missionaries, upon their return after the war, saw to it that he got proper medical care.

Today, though completely restored to mental and physical health, the scars remain, scars which are the handwriting of fiendish, Satan-inspired tormentors. In addition to the scars of torture, I saw with my own eyes his abdomen where seven operations were needed to repair the internal injuries caused when soldiers trampled him with their heels on the torturing ground.

Is it any wonder, now that God has restored him, that he ardently preaches the Gospel of Jesus Christ? I asked him, "How do you feel about it all now—as you look back upon so much suffering. Is it worthwhile?"

Radiance broke full across his face as he said, "Now my life is full of song. And I can tell my people about the joy of trusting Jesus. These are the real things in life. My only regret is that, during the banishment to Manchuria, I did not even then live consistently for my Lord."

With heroes such as this manning the helm, is it any wonder that the Korean church stands true?

CHAPTER FIVE

Sights Along the Way

White is a distinguishing color of Korea, for the first thing you notice when you come is the prevalence of white clothes. The farmer tramping through his muddy rice paddies, the workman in the shop and the factory, the coolie drawing the ricksha—all wear an almost uniform white garment. The old men, revered in the tradition of Oriental sagehood, wear long white robes.

Of course, an increasing number of the people, particularly young people and those who live in cities, wear western garb. Throughout the villages and the mass of Korea, however, the people pursue both toil and leisure in their white clothes.

I tried to find out why they wear white. It means that women must wash clothes more often, and I quickly noticed that one of the characteristic sights along the rivers and streams and wells is that of women scrubbing in the early morning and the late afternoon.

The passerby sees hundreds of women in their white clothes, little babies tied to their backs, kneeling at the side of a rock which serves as a scrub board. As the mother rubs her clothes, the head of the babe bounces back and forth as it tries to sleep.

I was told that the Japanese could not understand this custom, either. They tried to enforce a ruling whereby people were compelled to wear dark or at least colored garments. In fact, they went so far as to sit at the gates of the cities and villages and, as people came in, splash buckets of dye and paint onto the garments enough to mar them. People would then be forced to dye their clothes another color to keep them usable.

I finally discovered the reason for the white clothes. Back in the early days of Korean history, white clothing was adopted as the sign of mourning for the death of a king or relative or close friend.

Since the populace was often required to mourn the death of a monarch for as long as thirty years, the king had to begin his reign as a boy or be blessed with unusual longevity if his subjects were to have any change of style. So the men of the country, as a matter of course, adopted as their regular dress these gowns of white cotton over their baggy white trousers.

Soon after the beginning of Japanese rule in 1910, statistically minded Nipponese estimated that Korean women spent three billion hours a year washing white clothes. They also voiced the suspicion that Korean peasants worked less than Japanese because they were afraid of getting their white clothes dirty. So the Japanese launched a campaign to get the Korean men to wear dark clothes.

It failed.

They also tried, by the way, to force the Koreans to save fuel by feeding raw food to their farm animals. But the Korean farm wives went right on cooking meals for their bullocks and ponies.

Korea, with thirty million people, stands thirteenth in population among the nations of the world. However, like most of the Orient, its people live a sardine-can existence. The nation is forty-second in area among the nations of the world.

The peninsula, washed on three sides by salt water of the Japan Sea, the Korean Straight and the Yellow Sea, begins with a mountain peak called Peaktu in the far north. The name Peaktu means white head, explained by the fact that it is covered with glistening pumice. Peaktu is of volcanic origin, as are most of the mountains of the Orient, and in its ancient crater lies the deep and beautiful Dragon Prince's Pool.

Southeast from Peaktu runs the *Changpaik* range of mountains. Named because they are "ever white," this mountain backbone winds up and down the east coast to the very southern tip of the peninsula and, according to Korean folklore, has changed its direction. So rugged are these mountains, rising up out of the Japan Sea, that Korea's east coast has few good harbors.

On the western side of the peninsula the mountains slope gently into the sea, making numerous natural harbors. However, their seaworthiness is reduced by high tides. Inchon, the port of Seoul, for example, has twenty-nine foot tides—a factor carefully considered by U.N. forces when they staged their historic invasion.

Pusan has the best harbor. It was here, in 1592, that the Koreans sent a turtle-shaped ship, the world's first iron-clad vessel, to beat back invading Japanese.

Korea's northern mountains lie beautiful with snow from September till March. Rugged and heavily forested with spruce and larch and birch, juniper, maple and walnut, they are the wildland home for leopards, wild boars, wolves and tigers—animals ever a menace to the northern peasants.

In fact, tigers have been so much a part of north Korean life that the Chinese have a saying, "The Koreans hunt the tigers one half of the year, and the tigers hunt the Koreans the other half of the year." It is a fact that north Korea produces more tiger pelts than it does timber.

As the mountains spread southward, their forest covering gradually changes to pine and alder and then disappears entirely. As the forests disappear, the mountains become mere hills in the far south.

The climate, likewise, grows milder, and comes to resemble that of southern Virginia. In both north and south Korea, rainfall is almost entirely confined to July and August. This heavy concentration of precipitation is welcomed in the wide and fertile valley of the south, which contains three times as much rice paddy land as the north, and where two crops of rice, barley, wheat or rye go to the bins annually.

Essentially, nothing distinguishes the more than twenty million south Koreans from the nine million who inhabit the north. All speak the same language—a tongue not related to Chinese and Japanese but to Finnish, oddly enough, and Hungarian and Turkish. Koreans, however, usually write with Chinese characters.

The people of the north and the south eat the same food, relying heavily on highly spiced cabbage called *kimchi.* In physical appearance, also, there is little regional difference among the people. Somewhat taller than the Japanese on the average, they are nonetheless hard to distinguish from either the Japanese or Chinese.

This *kimchi,* by the way, adds a touch of local color to the Korean scene. For though poverty constantly broods over the large peasant and coolie populace, every farm house and every little hut—no matter what else the family's possessions might be—has huge earthen jars standing from two to four feet high, in which the national delicacy is kept.

Not only is this a characteristic sight, but also a characteristic smell! The stuff is made with peppery herbs, along with unspeakable quantities of garlic, and anyone who dares to eat it becomes atomic for days!

Another common sight is that of the little ponies, diminutive beasts of burden, who plod the nation's roadways. Highly prized for their ability to carry up to two hundred pounds, these animals trek as many as thirty miles a day through steep and precarious mountain passes—longer distances over more suitable roadways.

The traveler's attention is brought to them not because they are so numerous, necessarily, but because they are probably the least gentle of all beasts of burden in the world. Desperate fighters, they squeal and trumpet at the slightest provocation, and will attack each other on the road—ignoring their loads, which, in the fury of the ordeal, often smash into bits. When stabled, they are short-chained to troughs, preventing them from raising their heads. At night, I've been told, many of them are partially slung to heavy beams—to keep them from breaking into tantrums.

Even under these restricted conditions, they give vent to their temperament with hyena-like yells, and attempt to bite or kick.

Consequently, Korea's beast of burden receives hard treatment. I have seen them so brutally beaten in public that I was tempted to run and protect the animal.

Unfortunately, the *kimchi* jar and the tempestuous pony are not the only typical sights. Alcoholism holds a vicious grip on many of the men. I traveled with Andrew Gih and others over forty thousand miles throughout China, and I cannot remember ever seeing a drunken Chinese. You cannot walk down the streets of even the small villages in Korea, however, and not see men staggering under the influence of liquor. The Koreans, it seems, picked up the vice from the Japanese, who are great on the use of wines, beers and heavily intoxicating liquors.

Prostitution, too, reminds one that sin has put its roots deep into the scheme of these people's lives. As in other parts of the Orient, one can find girls on whose faces the look of innocence has not yet given place to the realization that they have become chattel to the leisures of hell.

Against the glorious spiritual story of Korea, there is the somber backdrop constantly reminding both the native Christians and the visitor that many yet wait to know the joy of forgiven sin.

CHAPTER SIX

A Trip by Korean Railroad

Arriving at Seoul's Kimpo airport, I was given a heart-warming reception in the home of the Kilbournes at the Seoul Seminary, a branch of the Oriental Missionary Society carried on by the Korean Holiness Church. Later, when Bob Findley joined me in Korea, he stayed at the Presbyterian compound with Harold Voelkel, Otto De Camp and Ned Adams, head of Presbyterian work throughout Korea.

The day following my arrival in Seoul, fifty-eight men —among them the bishop of the Methodist church, the presbyter of the Presbyterian church, pastors, missionaries and educational leaders—gave a reception.

That night, in Korea's largest church, I preached my first sermon. A unique church, pastored by Hanchun Zik who came to Seoul from North Korea with his entire parish after Communists took over above the 38th parallel, it was converted from a Buddhist temple, having a main floor and balcony which in America would accommodate about four hundred people. That night, however, no less than fifteen hundred people jammed the floor and balcony of the auditorium. The church had no pews, and the people huddled together in one great mosaic of human flesh.

God moved my heart with a new and unforgettable experience that night, as Pastor Hanchun stood and said, "Let us pray." Fifteen hundred people lifted their voices reverently and quietly—all of them praying aloud at once—in earnest outpouring of the petitions of their hearts to the Lord. After a few moments, the pastor tapped a little bell. The people finished their praying, by groups, then one by one, and when all was quiet the pastor offered a word of intercession.

I had never seen anything like this before, except among our Pentecostal brethren in America. This was a Presbyterian church, however, and I cannot forget how deeply it moved me as these dear Korean men and women, their faces lifted toward God as they sat there on the floor, poured out their hearts in concert prayer.

I was to see this kind of intercession throughout all South Korea.

My itinerary necessitated that this first visit to Seoul be short. The next day I boarded a train for Taegu, second largest city of Korea, some six and a half rail hours south of Seoul.

I found Korean railroads considerable improvement over those of China. Built by the Japanese, they offered comparative comfort as over against bumping along the rough roads. There are actually only some twenty or thirty miles of paved highway in all of Korea. A jeep trip of any length is always an agonizing ordeal.

As is true with most foreign railroads, the trains of Korea offered three classes of travel. First class is used only by wealthy folk, military and foreigners. The better class of merchants, as well as missionaries, usually ride second class. Third-class cars, comprising by far the largest number on every train, are packed and jammed beyond capacity. People cling in windows, doors and in vestibules. Oftentimes I saw them standing between cars, four or five people straddling precariously.

It is not an unusual thing to see as many as two hundred people jammed into one third-class railroad car in Korea.

We traveled by first class or second class, since the poorer people are so crowded in their compartments that they resent it if foreigners take up space in their cars when they could afford to ride where common people cannot.

Even when riding first class, however, I never came off an overnight trip or a day-long ride without having to battle with fleas. I don't know if they bother the Koreans much, but every time I got on a train it seemed as though one of the little *varmints* spread the news that here was a delicious variation of the ordinary diet.

Another discomfort is the tiny berths. The trains have been made for people of Japanese dimensions. Koreans are larger than the Japanese, but not quite as hulky as we Americans. Ceilings, too, are much lower, and so my memory of the Korean trains is that I could never stretch my legs clear out nor sit erect in the tiny little berths.

The evangelistic team of Bob Pierce and Bob Findley found eager hearts awaiting them in the midst of the rubble of war-torn Korea.

Top: School boys listen attentively to the Gospel.

Center: An improvised pulpit.

Bottom: An open-air auditorium.

CHAPTER SEVEN

The Gospel Preached

The first meeting in Taegu was held in the Presbyterian church. Though it was specifically for Christians (no other people invited except pastors and their congregations), over fifteen hundred jammed the edifice to the doors.

That night God led me to preach on the subject, "The Man God Uses," emphasizing the price it costs for a Christian to be mightily used of God. I'll never forget the hunger, the tears that came to their eyes and trickled down their cheeks as the meeting came to its close, and these people, many of whom had already suffered so much, lifted up their faces to God and cried out that He might help them to pay whatever the price might be to be used of Him.

For our evangelistic meetings we moved to the town hall, an auditorium seating around two thousand people.

At the outset, it was jammed to capacity with many young people in attendance, since it had been announced that Gil Dodds would be with me there, though he did not arrive until a few days later. That first night over a hundred people came forward in this hall, marched up the steps and onto the stage, and stood there publicly confessing that they were sinners seeking Christ as their Saviour.

Thus began that night a marvelous work, which in the course of nine weeks was to see the Spirit of God bring over twenty-five thousand people to the feet of the Lord

Jesus Christ in response to simple, straight-from-the-heart gospel messages and invitations.

From that night on, for the next eleven days, not a service passed without that auditorium being packed to capacity. Even when it rained, scores had to be turned away.

Those evening evangelistic services comprised only a part of the activity at Taegu, however. Let me, by way of example, lay out a typical day's schedule.

Up at 5:30, we made our way through the narrow, twisting streets of the city—through the pitch-black darkness preceding the dawn—to the First Presbyterian Church for the morning daybreak prayer meeting. Each morning, at crack of dawn, nearly a thousand people gathered to pour out their hearts in prayer. The service usually lasted an hour and a half. I would preach for a half hour or forty minutes, and the rest of the time would be spent calling on the Lord for a spiritual awakening in the city.

At seven-thirty, just after the prayer meeting finished, we grabbed a bite of breakfast. Then at nine, we would be in one of the public high schools of the city.

I remember one boys' school in particular. The principal told me that although he was not a Christian, he was much concerned for the fifteen hundred young chaps who comprised his student body. "Older people are too wise to be fooled by Communist propaganda," he said, "and that is why they prey upon the minds of young people. At this age young people are eager, and they are challenged by Communism."

Then, looking straight into my eyes, he said, "We want you to preach your Christ, because even though most of us on the faculty are not Christians, we know that only Christianity offers a challenge strong enough and stirring enough to turn these young people from Communism."

He not only wanted us to preach, but to give a Gospel invitation.

That morning nearly the entire student body of fifteen hundred jammed into the auditorium. There they stood fully fifty minutes while I presented the simple claims of the Gospel of Jesus Christ. Then I gave an invitation, wording it as clearly as I knew how through the lips of an excellent interpreter. Well over a hundred young men came to the front, publicly confessing their desire to know Christ as Saviour—even though they knew it meant considerable persecution from classmates not sympathetic to Christianity.

Following the dismissal of the student body, we spent half an hour giving the seekers additional information from the Word on how to trust Christ. We made arrangements for them to attend a Bible class, beginning the following week—using the promise that a free copy of the Gospel of John would be given to all who came, so that trained Korean workers could continue the work of leading these seekers deeply into a knowledge of Christ.

Following a school assignment such as this, we would go to another high school, again present the Gospel, and once more see scores openly confess Christ as Saviour.

By this time the morning would be spent, as much as five hours of it devoted to preaching and counseling.

The day was only beginning. In the afternoon, we would visit one or two girls' schools. Here again the results of the morning would be duplicated, with often more than a hundred girls signifying their desire to know Christ as Saviour.

Then each night we held the evangelistic services, so thrilling that though we were often at the point of exhaustion, we forgot our weariness as we watched God work in mighty power.

CHAPTER EIGHT

The Gospel Received

Our first Sunday in Taegu offered an opportunity which has gained added significance through the blood-spattered weeks that followed. Gil Dodds joined our party that day. At six in the morning, we drove out to an army camp on the city's outskirts. There we preached to the young ROCs who were to die nine weeks later, for this regiment suffered heavy casualties when the enemies of the north unleashed their terror.

Gil stirred the hearts of these lads in the chapel that morning. Standing before them as a living witness for Christ, plus the fact that as a track star he is known by every red-blooded youth in Korea, he held his audience in rapt attention. When the invitation was given, eighteen raised khaki-sleeved arms high, signifying a desire to trust Christ as Saviour.

I can see them yet, these lads. Eyes lighted with the sheer zest for living known to youth of all races and nations. Shoulders square. Sitting erect in typical military fashion. They were made of real stuff, those boys. How we thank God for the privilege of telling them about the Saviour before death silenced them along the 38th Parallel.

Later that morning I preached at the West Gate Presbyterian Church, of which Paul Myong is pastor. Mr. Myong helped inaugurate Youth for Christ work in Korea and represented his country at the first World Congress on Evangelism held in Beatenberg, Switzerland, back in 1948. He is one of the country's leading evangelical spokesmen.

Over a thousand people jammed the sanctuary. We had a wonderful service. I begged them to pray for our city-wide meetings, asking them to search their own hearts, and be willing to pay any price for revival. I'll never forget the way the meeting ended, with those dear Korean Christians weeping before God in prayer for the salvation of Taegu's unsaved throngs.

That afternoon we held an outdoor meeting in the courtyard of one of the Presbyterian schools. Between four and five thousand people came, with over three hundred responding to a clear-cut invitation to receive Christ as Saviour.

God had already begun to answer our morning prayers!

That night, back in the town hall, we again saw multitudes jam every area, with a great company responding to the invitation.

God gave us daily harvests there in Taegu, as we found each hour of the day crammed with activity. The climax of our campaign came the day Gil Dodds ran an exhibition race in the city's great stadium, a structure seating something like sixty thousand spectators.

Korea is a sports-loving nation, especially interested in track and field events. Elaborate preparations preceeded the occasion. City officials gave it their whole-hearted cooperation. The provincial governor joined in excellently. (This governor, by the way, is an earnest Christian. Night after night in Taegu's city hall I saw him come and kneel beside weeping penitents, pointing them to Christ.) Newspapers and radio stations provided top publicity. To top it all, students were dismissed from high school and came marching en masse!

Gil ran a fine race, setting a new track record. Then when the cheering had not quite died away, he stepped to the platform and told the crowd that the greatest joy of his life was not that of winning a race on a cinder track but of knowing and serving the Lord Jesus Christ. His testimony was tremendously effective.

Bob Findley, unusually annointed of God for the job he was to do those weeks in Korea, followed Gil with a half-hour message. From the moment he began I could sense the spiritual tenseness which had come over the audience. Bob has an excellent delivery, especially adaptable to work through a translator and geared to the thinking of youth. He spoke with force and tenderness.

In the weeks that followed Bob Findley never arose to speak without a hush of anticipation and respect sobering its way across the audience.

We could not possibly count the throng who responded to the invitation, much less get their names and addresses for proper follow-up. All we could do was pray for them and with them, doing our utmost to make sure that each of them understood what it meant to turn from the darkness of heathenism and unbelief unto the glorious light of the Gospel.

God gave us over twenty-five thousand decisions during our itinerary through southern Korea—a figure we mention merely to show the scope of the harvest— but this total does not include any decisions in meetings such as this where circumstances did not permit us to deal with seekers personally.

Reluctantly we left Taegu, a city in which we did not find so much as one missionary not absolutely true to the Word of God and the message of the shed blood of Jesus Christ. Howie and Del Moffat. Arch Campbell and his family. Bill Lyons. To us they became fountains of spiritual blessing. They cannot come to one's mind without the accompaniment of a prayer of gratitude to God.

CHAPTER NINE

Pusan

From Pyongyang to the Kremlin, Pusan has become a symbol of frustration. Because of Pusan, Mao Tse-tung reportedly went to bed with a bad case of neuro-gastric disturbances. Because of Pusan, plans for a spring invasion of Formosa did not materialize; pressure was relieved in Indo-China; Hong Kong could breathe a bit easier; and troops did not pour quite so relentlessly across the Tibetan border.

Its perimeter beachhead, held by General Douglas MacArthur and his heroic U.N. troops, proved once again to world tyrannists that freedom is not a dead concept in the hearts of men who have known its glory.

Yet, strangely, we did not find Pusan as warm to the message of the Gospel as was true in other cities south of the Parallel. Of the nine hundred full-size posters put up announcing that Gil Dodds would be there with me, over six hundred were deliberately torn down and destroyed by unknown antagonists.

However, God gave us five fruitful days in the city— particularly blessing the visits we made to schools.

I think I shall always particularly remember the fact that we spent Easter in Pusan, for on that morning it was my privilege to address a sunrise gathering atop a hill formerly the location of one of the most famous Japanese Shinto temples. On this spot, during World War II, Korean Christians had been forced at bayonet point to come and kneel. Many had faced death and imprisonment and indescribable torture rather than to deny their Lord. Consequently, this shrine had become to Christians in the Pusan area an emblem of persecution.

Days of horror lay in the past that morning, however, as members of the Church of Jesus Christ, which Satan had been unable to destroy, sang praises to the power of a risen Saviour!

No less than three thousand gathered that morning.

We sang "Christ Arose," the people in their language, we in ours. I did not know then what suffering awaited Korea. But remembering that my brethren had suffered where, where all lay now in complete tranquility, brought to my heart a profound moving of respect and reverence.

Here my God had permitted warriors of the Cross to prove the power of His name, the sustaining grace of His peerless love. I wondered, those soul-searching moments, if my faith would be strong enough to trust Him through such testing.

I wondered, and I bowed my head.

Then, just as the sun came stealing over the mountains, its rays breaking in golden glory across the city, I opened the Word of God and brought a message on the triumph of the empty tomb.

The following day was slated for another exhibition race by Gil Dodds. However, the city wanted to honor some of their crack troops just returned from guard duty at the 38th Parallel, and so at the request of city officials, we combined our meeting with the city's reception for these three thousand American-trained soldiers.

It proved to be another of the many providential arrangements we witnessed in Korea, for after the military ceremonies ended, fully thirty thousand people in addition to the troops, remained.

Gil ran an exhibition race, delighting young and old as he had done in Taegu, and then challenged them with a clear-cut testimony. The governor of the province, also a Christian, spoke a few words. Then it was my privilege to bring a message from the Word of God.

Those troops remained in Pusan for a week, after which they returned to the 38th Parallel. A few weeks later, sixty percent of those three thousand men became casualties of war. The only witness to the saving power of Jesus Christ most of them ever heard was the witness of that day in Pusan.

Their visit to Pusan was indeed a fitting climax to the meetings we held there.

CHAPTER TEN

Seoul

I was to see Seoul lie in ruins.

Before devastation struck, however, the city reminded me of a kind of Shanghai in Korea. Like the great Chinese metropolis, it stands slightly inland from the sea. Then, too, both mark the transition between Orient and Occident—their streets full of the thoroughfare of a modern world, yet marred by the heartache of paganism and embellished by the intrigue and color of the East. In Shanghai it was enterprising business men of an entire world who brought the modern touch. In Seoul the Japanese had constructed the wide avenues and modern buildings, where men in western business suits brushed elbows with robed sages and ragged coolies.

The city itself was the cardiac of South Korea, people and commerce flowing into it and out from it all along the granite hills overlooking the Han river.

I noticed a difference in the people of Seoul. They are city folk, even the poorer classes quite different from the country peasants who comprise seventy-five percent of the population.

Seoul and Shanghai shared yet another similarity. Multiplied thousands of refugees sought respite there from Red-held areas. Penniless, because the North Koreans would not permit them to carry possessions below the 38th Parallel, many of them foraged the streets like wandering dogs. Multitudes of them lived, and died, in the gutters and alley ways.

A few had been fortunate enough to obtain lodging in some discarded American army tents along the city dump. Others lived in caves dug in the ground. These huddled together during the winter months, human body against human body, the only source of warmth. Tuberculosis, and about every other kind of communicable disease, added to their misery.

The sight of them broke my heart.

On cold mornings it was a common sight to see scores of bodies lovingly laid out for disposal—the bereaved relatives not even having a place where a grave could be dug and thus compelled to depend upon authorities for some kind of decent interment.

The greatest tragedy was not their hunger, their suffering, their dying, however. The tragedy which tore constantly at my heart, and at the hearts of missionaries and Christian workers too short-handed to reach them, was the fact that these dear people had not had a chance to hear the only real message of hope a man can ever know. Surely hosts of these refugees would have turned to Christ, if only there had been tongues enough to tell them of His redeeming love. Hadn't they risked their lives, abandoned their possessions and jeopardized their futures for the prospect of a few weeks or months out of the reach of political bondage?

My heart aches to think of these people and of the fact that we did not do more to reach them for Christ.

But Seoul had its glorious story, too.

We saw God work in that city. At early morning prayer meetings, in school assemblies and at the evening evangelistic meetings, God showed us that *His hand is not shortened . . . nor His ear heavy* when the hearts of His people cry out for blessing upon the harvest.

When the Seoul campaign began, some fifty churches —Presbyterian, Methodist, Salvation Army and Korean

Holiness—gave their full cooperation in the city-wide evangelistic effort geared to the needs of the more than one million people living in the metropolis.

The site chosen for the meetings was a structure newly obtained by the Presbyterians for their Independence Memorial Church, intended as a national monument to Korean independence.

The pastor of the church, soundly evangelical, had served on the Youth for Christ board in the city and expressed great eagerness to have the location used for the meetings.

The congregation had built a temporary tabernacle, a rather make-shift affair, which seated over three thousand. It was quite drafty, the wind whistling through its frail bamboo supports. The pews were rice sacks placed on the dirt floor.

I wondered what the attendance would be.

On our opening night, more than three thousand jammed inside. Missionaries estimated that another crowd of nearly five thousand stood outside, unable to gain admittance.

My heart was particularly moved by the singing that night. As I listened to them lift their voices in concert prayer, I felt once more the strange moving of God's Spirit upon that country. These were hungry hearts, hungry for the Word of God.

I gave a simple message, and extended the invitation. Scores came to the altar, the deliberate earnestness of their purpose clearly written upon their faces, emblazoned in their eyes, and I was tremendously shaken by the realization that God was doing something in Korea.

I did not, of course, realize then that a merciful God was offering strength and hope to those who in so short a time would suffer and die.

After the benediction that first night in Seoul, I turned

to one of the pastors and said: "This is wonderful. Let's have a morning prayer meeting here."

"We already have one," he said, smiling. "Why don't you come in the morning?"

So I arose at five a.m. the next day. It was bitterly cold—snow had only left the streets of Seoul a few days before—and the tabernacle had no heat. Yet when I arrived in the pitch-black darkness preceeding dawn, not less than three thousand people had gathered for the prayer meeting! Hundreds had stayed all night, huddled with their Bibles and song books in anticipation of the morning!

I thought of my own beloved America. What could God do if people there cared as much for the souls of their fellow men?

Realizing that great things lay in store for the campaign, we got carpenters busy that day. They knocked out the back end of the tabernacle and built a small platform which made it possible for people inside to see while, at the same time, we could face the great courtyard outside.

Twelve thousand people came that night!

So it was for the next nine nights, with the attendance growing for every service. In fact, on the first Friday night, students from the Seoul Seminary of the Oriental Missionary Society stood at the gate and took an actual count of people who came in. They totalled sixteen thousand in attendance.

On Sunday night, we had fully twenty thousand!

One of the most heartening things I observed was the way Bible women and elders, along with students from the seminaries, had been organized as personal workers. Whenever we gave the signal for the invitation, they arose like a crowd throughout the congregation, and as the hundreds of seekers came to the altar, almost every one had a personal worker instantly at his side.

A thrilling sight!

Another factor was the excellent interpreters God gave us, here as throughout Korea. One of them—as saintly a man as I have ever met—was Pastor Chay, for many years head of the Korean Holiness Church.

A man of great personal devotion, Pastor Chay in 1949 had challenged his church with such a burden for reaching the people of the land that they built sixteen new churches during a twelve-month period, and supplied funds for a pastor in each of the churches.

This took great personal sacrifice, as few of the people had even what we Americans would call nominal incomes. Pastor Chay himself gave generously. He has a wife and two daughters, both of college age, to care for. Though his salary, by American standards below a relief allowance, barely took care of their needs, he voluntarily took a fifty percent cut in order to help his congregation win the lost.

He had already suffered much for the cause of Christ. Standing no more than five feet three inches in height, weighing little more than a hundred pounds, he was an indefatigable firebrand. Like many of his co-laborers, he, too, had been imprisoned by the Japanese for refusing to compromise his message.

He went with us gladly, week after week, as our interpreter. While I poured out my heart with the full energy of a man who weighs two hundred pounds, this little fellow stood at my side and matched word for word, actually adding fervor to the burden of my message as I spoke. He stood with me until the last word of the invitation had been given, staying on the job until the last word of personal work had been done.

I have many memories of Seoul, as I saw it then and as I was to see it later. But most vivid in my mind are the memories which remind me that God was there then, and that He had been there often before.

He was there then in our nightly meetings, at schools during the day. He was with us the night a young Communist came to Christ, and then stood up before the ten thousand people assembled and gave public confession of a murder he had committed only a few days before.

We had a great time in Seoul.

Our meetings were held in the very shadow of the famous old South Gate, a magnificent pile of architecture—sweeping, up-curved tile roof, layer cake stories of massive rock piled one upon another in a great bulwark against the erosion of time. As I watched multitudes come to Christ against the shadow of that gate, I thanked God that, at last, the gates were also open to the proclamation of the Gospel.

One of my most vivid memories of Seoul is the sight that greeted my eyes each time I stepped into the pulpit. It was a sight kindred to what we saw throughout South Korea, but never quite like in Seoul.

Always standing out in the crowds were the great mass of white-dressed women, their hair combed back into little severe knots at the back of their heads, their simple white gowns flowing tight against their necks and down against their shoe tops.

I always saw children in the crowd, too. They sat there by the hundreds, eagerly listening for any little story we might tell. They especially liked to hear of far-away America, of its radio and television and streamlined trains.

I remember the beauty and dignity of the old people, the many God-fearing matriarchs and patriarchs who came to pray and to leave the blessing of their reverently spoken amens upon each meeting. Especially the women. Their lives had known only severity and plainness, but those who knew the Lord had the glory of Heaven upon their faces.

How they loved the Word of God!

In Seoul we met with unusual response in the schools. We held daily meetings in the high schools, and never failed to see literally hundreds of decisions. It was a nightly thrill to see these students come and confess Christ publicly at our evangelistic services, and to bring along their unconverted friends to hear the Gospel.

I am convinced that God was preparing the city for the dark hours which lay ahead, when the country would be made a grim playground for a lost world's confused bayonet-pointed politics.

Amid the ruins of war-torn Korea, children still enjoy the childish pastime of writing in the sand.

Korean youth is thirsty for knowledge. Books are highly-prized possessions and the ability to read much sought after.

Wherever Bob Pierce and his evangelistic team went they were greeted by vast crowds such as these. The Korean people are hungry for the Gospel and the things of God.

CHAPTER ELEVEN

A Modern Exodus

I met God's choisest saints in Korea.

They had come through great testing, these people. No wonder I found the texture of their faith so finely woven. No wonder I so constantly found myself feeling embarrassment, as I realized what they had done for the Lord in comparison to the scant service I, and so many of my fellow Christians back in America, have offered in appreciation of Calvary.

It is neither wise nor easy to classify these Korean saints, much less take from their midst any one and acclaim him as the greatest of all. But I do think that no one I met in Korea so clearly illustrates the stature of these God-fearing believers as Hanchun Zik, pastor of the Presbyterian church in Seoul where we saw such glorious blessing bestowed from the hand of the Lord.

A man of slight stature, his pastoral program would stagger any clergyman I know in America. Never less than twelve, and often as many as eighteen, hours of every day he spent tirelessly carrying on his program of evangelism. Even so, he found time to serve gladly as my interpreter in many of the meetings as well as on the occasion when it was my privilege to address the General Assembly of the Presbyterian Church.

I saw Hanchun Zik minister to the multitudes, caring for men's souls irregardless of their station in life. I watched him mete out mercy to refugees. I marveled at the depth of his patience as he grappled with the personality problems peculiar to the Orient. Hour upon hour I watched him.

My head bowed in shame and reverence. For I knew that, like so many of his fellow citizens, he constantly battled the tuberculosis germs which fevered his body.

Before coming to Seoul, Pastor Zik pastored a large work north of Parallel 38. When the Communists took over, it seemed that he would be able to continue unhindered, for they offered their usual cordiality at first, promising not to interfere in any way with the work of the church.

Gradually, though, restrictions elbowed their way into freedom of liberty and worship until Christian enterprises became next to impossible. Pastor Zik read the handwriting on the wall. His was a large work; consequently, it would provide a fine target for atheistic forces wishing to illlustrate their technique in completely strangling the message of the Gospel.

Those were harrowing days. People began to disappear—taken from their homes in the middle of the night, going to work and never returning, picked up and imprisoned on suspicion or because they allegedly spoke or acted unfavorably against the new regime.

Christians particularly began to know the gnawing fear that at any hour of the day or night they or their dearest loved ones would be arrested because of some uncompromising stand manifested in behalf of the Gospel.

The church went underground. Home prayer meetings took the place of congregational worship. But the people bore the mark of Christ, and it became increasingly difficult for them to go about even their workaday employment.

As the tension mounted, people began to look southward, willing to pay almost any price for the freedom of worship they once had known. Family after family began to investigate the possibility of moving below the Parallel.

Hanchun Zik spent hours in prayer those days. He could face suffering, should it be the price of blessing. But he did not want his efforts to be so completely decimated that, as has so often become the case under Red domination, it would be impossible to do anything in the way of spiritual service.

Finally, sure in his heart of the will of God, he began to counsel with his people. He had a plan.

Short weeks later, the pastor and almost his entire congregation left North Korea and set out across the long and winding mountainous miles. Often they blazed new trails, in an effort to cross the 38th Parallel without being apprehended by authorities.

Many, of course, did not succeed. As they congregated near the border, preparatory to the final dash across, families split up. A father would take part of a family, his wife the remaining children. Or some of the children might go with a third group. In this way, they reasoned, no entire family would be likely to perish.

So it was that, when families began to regroup on the other side, many of them heard agonizing accounts of how their loved ones had faced almost instantaneous execution when apprehended by Communist authorities. Others were made prisoners—the men, whose stature gave promise of value in labor camps, the women, whose fair youth would be plunged into a fate worse than death.

Two years had passed when I heard this modern Exodus story, and the church was still supporting over one hundred and fifty orphans, all of whom had lost their parents in the migration out of the north.

There were other prices these Christians had to pay. They had taken with them only such few possessions as their hands could carry—not much, considering the fact that supplies of food had to be brought lest they find none along the way, or be forced into extended hiding in the hills.

So they had entered Seoul poverty-stricken.

Pastor Hanchun Zik rose to the occasion with all the wisdom of a patriarch. Soothing his people with the ministry of the Word, he set about to organize them into cooperatives. A plot of ground, which he was able to secure on the edge of the city, was proportioned to the men, who set about preparing the soil. From relief agencies, he obtained enough seed for planting.

He kept the women busy, too, making clothes out of the scraps and rags he managed to secure.

Administrators were set up among the flock to see that everything was equally divided, that everyone had an equal opportunity. The most nourishing food went to the sick, the warmest clothing to the frail and feeble. Heaviest chores were done by the strong, hand-strength work by those whose shoulders could not lift heavy burdens.

Nothing was overlooked. Pastor Zik secured used and improvised tents, and organized a school. Women who could not work in the fields looked after a nursery for the children of mothers who could work in the fields. Those with academic training taught in the school.

He located a bombed-out factory, once used to manufacture tennis shoes, the Orient's predominant footwear. Blazing the way with his own bare hands, he reclaimed enough scrap wreckage to get the plant going again, and in a year's time—during our visit at the factory— one hundred families in his church earned their bread and shelter from this source.

Thus, out of the chaos of the past, this man of God built a future for his people.

One thing lacked, however. They needed a place of worship. So Pastor Zik went to government officials and pled for the use of an old Buddhist temple. This he converted into a place of worship, and it was still used at the time of our visit—for on one occasion, I preached to no less than fifteen hundred people within its walls.

Naturally, the congregation grew. Others came down from the north, and were added to the number. But most of all, the people had hearts aflame for the souls of their countrymen. Twice each Sunday morning the church was filled to capacity, with many finding Christ at almost every service.

Among Christians like those we met in Korea, Han-chun Zik is an example, not an exception.

CHAPTER TWELVE

Supreme Love for the Lost

I must tell you of one other hero, for he so aptly typifies the zeal Korean Christians have for winning the lost. He served as pastor of a Seoul church. When I heard his story, I understood why so many of these Korean clergymen withheld church membership from new converts unless they, too, had won others to Christ.

I had read a brief account of this man's story in *Time* magazine back in America, and so it became all the more pleasing to meet him personally.

Like Hanchun Zik he was slight of stature. There was a gentleness about him which made it hard to believe that he had suffered unmentionable tortures at the hands of the Japanese during World War II.

When the decree had gone out that all Koreans must bow at the Shinto shrines, he had willingly made himself a public example in order to encourage members of his flock as well as other believers. Fully expecting to lose his life, he became instead one of the living martyrs— those to whom the conqueror forbid the mercy of death.

If only God could somehow let every Christian in America see this man's scars!

He had two sons. Like all Korean fathers, they were his greatest treasures. It was they who would carry his name to succeeding generations.

That was his dream.

As World War II came to a close, and peace brought a temporary quiet to the land, these sons were just coming into manhood. Promise and hope dawned in the future. These boys knew their father's God. There was hope that they could serve Him in spiritual prosperity.

Peace had come to Korea. No, only the guise of peace, for international Communism began its infiltration program immediately, and the wake of the battleship *Missouri* had scarcely disappeared from the ship's armistice mooring off the Japanese mainland before organized Red front groups began their efforts to bring South Korea, like North Korea, under Kremlin control.

The chief targets were the schools.

In the school where this pastor's sons were training, preparatory to entering seminary, Trojan-horse Communism struck with all of its crafty, underhanded fury. Against its tide stood scores of earnest, uncompromising Christian students, like the pastor's two sons.

Not only did they stand against the enemy, but they launched a crusade to evangelize their fellow students. They did not act belligerently. Instead, they wanted only that the joy they knew in Christ might be shared by others who had not yet seen, as they had seen, what God could do in a young life.

So successful was their witness that officials underground dispatched a warning, an ultimatum that unless they discontinued their Christian activities among students they would face violent consequences.

They were in the royal line of martyrdom, these boys. Nothing mattered apart from doing what they knew God wanted them to do.

Their answer to the ultimatum was to witness more aggressively than they had ever done.

The consequences came.

A young Communist student, drunken with the emotional wine of a movement which is literally the fanatical evangelism of hell, was appointed to murder them. He succeeded, but before he could make his escape, he was arrested.

News of his sons' death nearly broke the father's heart. He went to his knees, and to the Book he loved, pleading for strength to endure and wisdom to understand.

Shortly after the funeral, he visited the murderer of his two boys, finding the young Communist a bewildered lad who knew nothing of the love of God.

"You will get your revenge," the lad said. "I have been sentenced to die."

The grief-stricken father did not want revenge, however. Instead, he went to the authorities and pleaded for leniency in behalf of the murderer.

"Don't put him to death," he begged. "Turn him over to me. The boy has never known love. My own sons might have fallen prey to such a godless philosophy, had they not been taught the ways of the Lord. Let me adopt this young Communist, as my own son."

Dumbfounded, the officials went into conference. Although they had already sentenced the youth for execution, they could not overrule such a tremendous demonstration of Christian love. They turned the boy over to the pastor.

Love, the first he had ever known, mellowed the young man's heart. He was gloriously converted, his life completely transformed by the tremendous power of the Gospel. While I was in Korea, I visited the Bible school where he had gone to prepare for the ministry!

Do you wonder why I returned to America with a new flame in my heart, a determination to make my own life count more for God and to do all I can, to make my fellow Christians see that nothing short of my all is enough for my Lord?

CHAPTER THIRTEEN

Taejon

It was at the close of the Seoul campaign after a quick visit to the Presbyterian General Assembly in Taegu, that we visited President Syngman Rhee. The next day we left by train for Taejon.

When we were there, the city's fame had cast but a faint glow beyond the borders of the land. In the soon-coming crucial struggle between tyranny and freedom, however, the city was to find its way into the vocabulary of every American who scans the front page of a newspaper.

Taejon is a pleasant city, thatched and tiled roofs telling of the old Korea and the modern ways brought by the Japanese. Its wide streets speak of the new world, but, strangely, we found few modern buildings.

I remember those wide streets, and they are like a blur in my memory. For when I think of them as they looked on that initial visit, teeming with people and the commerce of an Oriental thoroughfare, I am always reminded that—not long after the first visit to Taejon—I was to see on those streets the gory scars of a terrible war.

Ever since the beginning of Christian missions in Korea, Taejon has been known as a hard city. Famous as a center for Buddhism, it casts on the Christian who enters it a feeling of strange depression.

There had never been a united evangelistic crusade in the city's history. We went there with fear and trembling.

53

Taejon had seven Presbyterian churches, five Methodist churches, two or three Korean Holiness churches and a Salvation Army citadel. There was only one foreign missionary family, Mr. and Mrs. George Adams.

Mr. and Mrs. Adams arranged for us to stay with the United States military advisory group, encamped just outside the city. The week while we were there to preach, we had the privilege of eating our meals with U.S. officers and sleeping in the U.S. Army guest house.

It was a delightful privilege, so far from home.

Taejon has a large agricultural school, an engineering school and several high schools. Our meetings were scheduled to be held in the auditorium of one of those high schools.

The first night, the lights failed. Yet, as Bob Findley brought the message, souls came to Christ.

We did not remain in that auditorium. It could only accommodate about two thousand people, so we moved out into the school courtyard and set up a small platform and a public address system.

Night after night, crowds of five and six thousand people came and sat on the ground on rice mats as we proclaimed the Word to them.

They were not as easily handled as the crowds in Seoul. The children had an idea that we were some sort of traveling circus, and at the outset, they acted accordingly. This being a Buddhist center, they knew nothing of a worship service, let alone reverence in such a service.

Asking God for wisdom, we taught our congregation what was expected of them, and in a wonderful way God breathed His spirit upon those who sat before us. By the close of the campaign, we had their undivided attention.

We serve a great God. Night after night, He gave

the strength needed to proclaim His majesty. During the day, Bob Findley, Harold Voelkel, Mrs. Kilbourne and I ministered in the schools.

It moves me deeply now, thinking back. In God's kind providence—certainly nothing can be credited to our merit—we had the privilege of telling the people of that great Buddhist city that only in Christ is there hope. Soon after these meetings, the city was burned almost to the ground. Thousands of those children were robbed of their homes, hundreds of them slain along with their elders.

We have confidence, in the promise of a Word which will not return void, that we shall again meet multitudes of those who were snatched into eternity.

CHAPTER FOURTEEN

Kaesong

After the Taejon campaign, Harold Voelkel took us in his station wagon on a trip which was to be made more memorable with the passing of time. As we traveled hour after hour over the rough Korean roads, Harold spoke often of the blessing the station wagon had been to his ministry. It had been supplied by a church in Berkeley, California.

Our journey took us to Kaesong, another Korean city soon to be made famous by infamy. Kaesong stands almost directly on the 38th Parallel.

We met some Christian officers of the South Korean army who graciously offered to be our hosts. By an odd coincidence, we were just in time to witness the wake of an incident which pointedly illustrated the seething unrest along the Parallel.

Only two hours before our arrival a major in the North Korean army had slipped across the lines and had surrendered himself to the South Korean forces. He had attended school with officers of the South Korean army, had turned Communist and now, allegedly, wanted to be forgiven.

We were allowed to see this young man, and I can never forget the bewilderment written all across his face. His eyes were so full of fright that I could not try to call him guilty or innocent. I could only pity him—not because rumors were that he was to be executed, lest he should serve the Reds as a spy by posing as a repentant enemy, but because he so painfully illustrated the awful spiritual vacuum which exists when Communism moves in to areas where we, whom God has commissioned to do the job of evangelism, have not brought the message of hope in Christ. I wondered if I, or if some Christian back in America who had taken God's second best in life, could not have reached him for Christ before he lost his way so completely.

A lieutenant was assigned to go with us through the city of Kaesong, back up a rocky, unbelievably steep and narrow little road, which was the only way of getting to the last defenses of the South Korean army.

Up and up we went, dropping into chuck holes and bounding over jutting rocks until, at last, the car could go no farther. We got out, and walked the remainder of the way. Only a jeep or a tank could have traveled where we walked.

Suddenly we came around a corner of the mountain. There, carved out among the rocks, was the last outpost on the 38th Parallel—pill boxes and dugouts which were almost invisible until one actually stood among them.

Through the centuries, this spot had come to be known as a traditional invasion point. Invaders from China, Japan and Mongolia had moved across these rocky steeps. For to enter or leave South Korea, an army must march through passes in the mountains such as this one.

Such as this one?

Weeks later, when North Korean Communist forces plunged the dagger of their military might into the back of South Korea, the initial thrust was through this very pass.

Missionaries were in the Kaesong area at the time. They have not been accounted for.

Although I did not realize what was so soon to take place along the Parallel, pity again came to my heart. The armaments of these men were almost ridiculously inadequate. How could they ever hope to withstand an enemy of any competence?

About 150 soldiers were on duty at this post, and the commanding officer quickly called them together. They sang hymns with us, and stood in quiet reverence as we ministered briefly out of the Word of God and offered prayer.

God bless those men, if they have not already spilled their blood in defence of their country. And of my country. They stood there, gripping their guns, and as I told them of the Great Commander, they listened in rapt attention. Through the firing slits of that little fortress where we met, pill-boxes of Communism were in full view.

Thinking back now, I believe those men sensed that they were living on the brink of death.

Following the service, we made a brief inspection tour of the area. We took care to crouch low as we hurried from place to place. In this same fortress area, during the twelve preceding months, seven men had been killed by sniper fire from across the Parallel.

I did not learn that until a bit later, and I asked, "Why so many precautions? There's no one in sight over there on the other side of the Parallel."

Almost curtly, one of the men said, "Did you notice the ruined building along the streets of Kaesong as you came up?"

"Yes, I did," I told him. "I realized it had been bombed, but I thought that might have been quite sometime ago."

"Only a few weeks ago," he told me. "It was knocked to shambles by mortar shells lobbed over this mountain." Then he told me of men in their group who had been killed by the constant sniping and periodic bursts of rifle and machine gun fire.

The caldron was beginning to boil. Three days after our visit, five men were killed at the very spot where I had preached. Only weeks later, inferno itself was to break loose, as the molten fury of hate and heroism poured first into and then out of this pass.

As I stood there that day, I wondered how many had lost their lives in battle upon the very rocks where we walked. Today I wonder all the more. Of those who so lately have had to die, are there not those who would have listened to the message of redemption —as men in the pill box listened—if someone had brought that message to them?

CHAPTER FIFTEEN

A Korean Saint of God

In Korea, as throughout all of the Orient, women have a cumbersome lot in life. Perhaps that is why one finds so many of them who, when they become Christians, radiate the glory of God in every aspect of their lives. While they may yet be restricted by social limitations, their spirits have been set free in the liberty Christ alone can give.

While we were in Taegu, I stayed at the home of some missionaries who had an unusually fine cook. I'll never forget the wonderful rolls she baked each morning for breakfast. And I'll never forget her amazing story.

I learned that she had six children, all of whom she had put through school with the toil of her own hands, for her husband had been incapacitated years before. When we were in Taegu, this woman's last son had just finished college and was ready to enter medical school.

From the moment of their birth, she had literally bathed each of these children in prayer. You see, this woman realized what a difference there is between Christianity and heathenism. What a vast difference!

Born into a typical Buddhist home out in one of the country villages, the name of Jesus never fell upon her ears during her entire childhood. She had heard vaguely of missionaries, and was told to fear them as one fears death itself.

Life had a mingling of joy in it. Her parents showed her kindness. They lived above the rank-and-file poverty of the land. Her greatest joy came, however, when her parents told her she was to marry a wealthy young man.

The gods had looked upon her with great favor, they told her, to bring about such fine fortune.

Lavish preparations were made. Finer clothes than she had ever dreamed of owning were custom sewn for the great occasion.

Of course, she had not met her appointed bridegroom. In true Oriental fashion, the nuptial contract had been let without her consultation. But, knowing little else than the custom of her people and in true filial respect, she was not unhappy.

Finally, the eve of the wedding day arrived. The bride-to-be's clothes were given a final check, to make sure everything fitted her and the occasion to perfection.

An elderly woman stepped into the home to watch the excitement. She came into the room where the girl, alone, looked over her trousseau. The old woman's eyesight was failing, and because the girl made no noise, she thought the room was empty.

"What a pity," the old woman muttered, scarcely above a whisper. "All this preparation for an extravagant wedding, and the poor girl thinks she's getting a bargain. What a tragedy it is she doesn't know that the wealthy man she's about to marry is a leper."

Horror struck the girl's heart. A leper! She had been offered in marriage to a leper!

Unquestionably her parents knew. But they had weighed the matter carefully, and had decided that the wealth and prestige gained would be worth the price of their daughter's future.

Immediately the girl began to make plans for an escape, knowing she could expect neither pity nor mercy from anyone. Under the shelter of darkness, wearing many of the garments which had been prepared for her wedding, she slipped out of the house. With every ounce of her strength, she scaled the wall leading to the alley.

Darting from shadow to shadow she made her way out of the village and into the fields before her flight was known. She staggered through ditches and across rice paddies, not knowing where to go.

The entire village was thrown into an uproar—by those who resented the brass of a girl who would act this way, whatever the reason, and by those who welcomed the excitement.

Groups set out from the village, hunting for her. Through the night, she heard their cries, but evaded them. By dawn, she had gone beyond their reach.

She knew she dare not seek refuge in another village, for word of her act spread quickly. The price of generations was upon her head, and searchers were dispatched to all the surrounding villages. Then the girl thought of something.

The despised missionaries. Maybe they would help her. It was worth a try, she reasoned, as she made her way toward one of the mission compounds.

There she poured out her heart to the sympathetic ears of Christians who immediately loved her. The missionaries promised to give her refuge. They took her in and clothed her and then, in the secrecy of another night, moved her to another compound some thirty miles away.

For two years, the girl was moved from one mission compound to another, in order to hide her from the constant search carried on for her. Perhaps by the end of those two years, the man she was to have married would have rejected her, but her own relatives sought her, feeling completely justified to punish her actions severely because of the deep embarrassment brought upon them. The girl adjusted herself to service as a servant in the various missionary homes which gave her shelter, and in the course of time, the love of these people won her heart. In the simple but sure act of faith, she trusted Christ as her personal Saviour.

Shortly after this she came to one of the missionaries and said, "I'm just a poor girl now, and I don't have anything to give in return for what you have done for me. But I have the future ahead of me. I am well and strong. I want to serve the Lord."

Her consecrated youth became a vivid witness for Christ.

Before many years passed, she met a young Christian lad. They were married. Then tragedy struck, for the husband was rendered incapable of supporting his family. She would not accept defeat, however.

Each of her children was educated, supported by her twelve to sixteen daily hours of toil. Each of them finished at the head—or near the head—of his class. How proud she was of them.

I met the last boy, her youngest son. His proud mother, now wrinkled with age, brought him to me. "He has finished college," she said, "and now we want him to attend medical school. Please pray that God will supply the need. I know you are a man of prayer, because God has used you so greatly in Korea. School begins in three days at the Severns Medical Hospital in Seoul, but he has no money."

She was silent a moment, and so was I.

"He has dedicated his life to God," she told me, "to be a medical missionary here in Korea."

"How much does it cost for him to attend medical school?" I asked.

Her eyes widened, and she shook her head sadly. "It is a vast sum," she said. "It costs so much we dare not talk about it to ourselves. We only bring it to God."

I asked the missionary, who was interpreting our conversation, how much a year's medical training would cost.

"For a year," the missionary told me, "his room, board and tuition would run about thirty dollars per semester—sixty dollars a year."

Using funds which Christians back in America had entrusted to me, I made arrangements for this chap to get his medical training. When the dear mother understood, she looked up at me with eyes full of tears and wonderment. Somehow, my eyes, too, were filled with tears.

CHAPTER SIXTEEN

A Korean Bible Conference

American Christians need no introduction to the Bible conference idea. A good many of them, however, who vacation at a Bible conference each summer, would find it difficult to believe that the one Bob Findley attended in Korea actually existed.

High in the mountains of South Korea, more than a thousand Christians gathered to seek the face of their God.

Housing proved no problem. There was no rush for the best accommodations, no complaint over facilities or room costs. Drenching rain fell, but no one complained. They had chosen this place of beauty not for diversion but for seclusion.

The sky was the only roof they had.

Nor did they complain about the food. For, there on the mountain top, they fasted, spending all their time in prayer and in the counsel of the Word!

It may not be easy for you to believe what Bob saw. It was not easy for him to believe. Bob Findley is the kind of chap the American vocabulary calls "sharp." Collegiate—he was a boxing champion at the University of Virginia—and extremely discerning, Bob has a warm heart for the Gospel, but all the same, he is not one to be easily swept by reports he has not had a chance to verify. Here, and at meetings like this, God showed this young man the might of His outstretched arm.

A paralytic boy was brought to this mountain retreat. He came that he might feast upon spiritual manna. But he came for yet another reason. He came because God had ordained to reveal His power through this lad.

There was a tremendous stirring of spiritual power at that particular prayer meeting. It was not a meeting called to pray for the sick, but a meeting where men and women cried out to God for blessing and salvation upon the land.

Yet, in the midst of that prayer meeting, this boy leaped to his feet. Like the man who sat at the temple gate in Acts 3, he was instantly healed.

"It was incredible," Bob Findley told me. "I saw him earlier and his right foot and arm were hopelessly disabled. He had been carried to the gathering on the back of a relative. When I saw him standing, I could hardly believe my eyes. So I walked over to the lad, touched his flesh and found it vigorous and firm."

In that same meeting, a man who had been dumb for forty years was miraculously healed. "I heard him speak," Bob says, "and I saw the wonderment on the faces of those who realized how great was that miracle."

Nearby stood a mother, weeping for joy. Beside her stood a young man, excitedly picking up objects with his right hand—a hand which had previously been withered beyond use.

You don't believe it? Then my friend Bob Findley is a liar. I, too, am a liar, for manifestations of this kind happened again and again, under the tremendous impact of a people who cared neither for time nor food nor personal comfort when they set out to pray for the annointing of God's Spirit upon their lives and ministry.

Do you wonder why I have such an overpowering love for these dear people? They are my seniors in the Gospel! They walk with God in a fellowship which

I yet long for! To think that they yet cry out so hungrily for more of His power!

After I had witnesed some of these things, it was not difficult to believe that there is not a more vigorous church on the face of the earth. No wonder the Koreans, differing from all the Orient, sent missionaries to fellow lands like China. No wonder the Korean church is so staunchly indigenous.

In fact, I firmly believe that the job of pastoring the congregations can now rest completely in the hands of the native workers. Foreign missionaries in Korea can devote their time to improving methods, to provide theological training, to dispensing guidance.

Evangelists from abroad are needed to bring the driving force of the Occident. I have prayed earnestly, during the awful see-saw back and forth among the U.N. troops and the Reds, that God would rid the land of war and with that blessed situation burden the hearts of scores of America's leading evangelists to go and harvest in Korea.

For it is harvest time there.

CHAPTER SEVENTEEN

Inchon

Communist troops, riding the wild wave of success in their June 1950 initial assault, swept the city into the net of their strategy as soon as possible. They needed Inchon.

As port of Seoul—the two cities are linked by twenty-five miles of the only good pavement we found in the country—it served as a key supply port for American troops during the days of occupation following World War II.

With Seoul completely strangled by the possession of Inchon, the Reds needed only to push U.N. forces back to and out of Pusan to have the country completely dominated by the hammer and sickle.

Only a few days before the bloody surprise attack, we conducted our concluding "Save the Nation" evangelistic campaign in the city. In many respects, this finale to the intinerary proved the most successful. I tremble to think that we might have let the blessings of Inchon pass us by.

The meeting was held at the request of native pastors, who sent a delegate to Seoul to plead our coming. At first, we refused. We were dog tired. Inchon had not been on the original itinerary. More than that, by this time we had invested—in campaign expenses, for literature used in advertising and convert follow-up, through needy projects which constantly presented themselves—the funds we had brought from America.

We were broke. In fact, we had not only exhausted

our budget but had used our return fare to purchase some last minute Scripture portions urgently needed and to care for other costs directly related to the job of evangelism in South Korea.

Obviously, it fell to our lot to carry almost the entire burden of finances in the campaigns. War-ridden Koreans lived on a daily economy which made it impossible for them to do much in the way of monetary help, a condition which they more than equalized by the tremendous cooperation and tireless toil and unceasing prayer which they literally poured into the work.

We stated the situation frankly to the Inchon clergy.

"We'll trust God," they told us. "He will supply the need. Our city has not had a spiritual awakening for many years, and there has never been a city-wide effort to our knowledge. You must come. God must do for Inchon what He did in Seoul and in these other cities."

It would have been gross spiritual disobedience to give a negative answer to such a plea!

"All right," I told them. "You set up the meetings. If you're willing to pay the expenses involved in publicity, then we'll make arrangements to pay our own expenses and come."

The meeting place was the Methodist church, largest in the city, with seating accommodations for about twelve hundred people.

At the first service, held in the morning, people jammed every inch of space in the auditorium. That night we could not begin to get the crowd inside. Public address equipment, set up in the courtyard, accommodated the estimated eight thousand who failed to get in. They not only jammed the courtyard but spilled over and clogged the little alley running from the courtyard to the street.

At the invitation, scores came weeping to the altar, as the great week's harvest got underway.

My heart cried out in gratitude to God for the realization that His Spirit was again outpoured, and I again became deeply conscious of the fact that we had come in the sovereign will of God. He was going to do something for the city.

I did not, of course, realize then that so many of those who heard the Gospel through our ministry, and who came to a knowledge of Christ as Saviour, would meet violent death upon the streets of the city.

I was to return to Inchon and find the landmarks, which came to be so familiar to us, reduced to rubble. Inchon, fair city by the sea. Here General Douglas MacArthur—the old soldier whose greatness and wisdom shall not fade away, whose convictions on strategy for the Orient shall someday be vindicated—was to launch the thundering counter-offensive against Moscow from which the reeling Reds would never fully recover. Here dope-crazed North Koreans were to make their suicide charges, and fall dead in the street, their passing of no more incident to their leadership than the expenditure of so much irreplacable ammunition.

My heart cries out in gratitude to God for having had a part in preparing His people at Inchon for disaster, and above all for the privilege of sowing the Word among multitudes of hearts where otherwise the shrouded future could have known no dawn.

CHAPTER EIGHTEEN

A Modern Joshua

Inchon was to be a finale in many respects.

It concluded our intinerary. It was perhaps the last evangelistic effort conducted in South Korea before terror struck. It also became something of a summing up of spiritual blessing.

We held a six o'clock Bible study and prayer meeting each morning. Morning after morning, twelve to fifteen hundred people jammed the Methodist church to capacity. There in the pitch-black darkness, they listened eagerly to the Word, and poured out their hearts for the blessing of God.

Is it any wonder we saw God's hand manifested?

At eleven each morning we held a meeting exclusively for Christians. One morning, at the beginning of the campaign, I preached on the dangers of sin in the lives of Christian workers. Over a hundred pastors and Bible women that morning publicly confessed their sins and their desire to be right with God.

Is it any wonder we saw God's hand manifested?

At these eleven o'clock meetings, we made arrangements for the care and follow-up of converts. It was a joy to see how the pastors worked in complete unanimity. One did not bicker with another over who should be given the most names as possible additions for his flock. Instead, there was a concord of heart to see to it that each convert received the proper spiritual nurture during the initial weeks so important to his spiritual development.

I say, is it any wonder we saw God's hand manifested? Each afternoon we ministered in the schools. God keeps the record, and to Him belongs all the glory, but there were days when we had as many as twelve hundred students publicly make known their desire to trust Christ as Saviour.

Let me emphasize, lest anyone be critical. We did not keep tabulations so that, like some sort of spiritual big game hunters, we could return to America with glowing reports of how we came and saw and conquered. God forbid!

Having witnessed such unusual working of the Spirit of God, we can hardly be blamed for speaking our enthusiasm. We do not know, for example, how many of these high school and college students came to a personal knowledge of Christ as Saviour and Lord in their lives. We do know that we made the message as clear as possible, the invitation as definite as possible, and that among those with whom we counseled personally, we found a great hunger for salvation.

With an overflow crowd of eight thousand estimated at our opening service, it became necessary at the outset to secure more sizable accommodations.

There was no other auditorium in the heart of the city, however, which held more than the church. We sent men out to investigate. We questioned everyone we could think of who might offer a solution. All our efforts proved fruitless.

Then someone got an idea. The railroad station. A large open area flanked the terminal building. Checking, we discovered that the last train left each evening at 8:20. The meetings could be held without disturbance after that.

We secured police permission and announced that all meetings at night would be held in the largest space of the courtyard directly in front of the station.

Bob Findley spoke at the eleven o'clock meeting next morning, held in the church. He found many of the Christians distressed. "The meetings will be ruined," they said. "This is the time of heavy rain. Once rainfall begins, it will continue uninterrupted for days and days."

God filled that young man's heart with boldness as he stood to speak to those dear people. "You told us you would trust God to meet the needs," he said. Cautiously, he added, "Let us trust Him now."

Outside, it had begun to rain. Now, as Bob spoke, a torrential downpour swept against the windows of the church.

Then he told of an experience Dr. Charles Fuller had had back in an Iowa city, when rain beating upon a metal roof threatened to make broadcasting impossible. "Dr. Fuller bowed his head, and asked God to stop the rain," Bob told the people. "And five minutes before the Old Fashioned Revival Hour broadcast was to begin, the rain stopped. I believe with all my heart that God will stop this rain in time for us to hold the meeting outdoors tonight. Tell everyone you can that God is going to roll back the clouds, and give us fair weather tonight."

His concluding statements had the accompaniment of a furious burst of rain.

It was twelve-thirty noon when Bob raced out of the church and through the downpour into the car which took him to our hotel room. Together, we got on our knees and—crying out for faith to dispel our unbelief —trusted God to withhold the storm.

"You did it at Galilee, Lord," we prayed. "Joshua spoke, using divine authority, and the sun stood still. You did it for Dr. Fuller back in America. Now, Lord, it is human foolishness to believe that, right in the heart of the rainy season, the skies will clear. But we believe the miracle will happen, bringing glory to the name of our God and the Lord Jesus Christ."

At 2:30, a wind arose. By 3:00, the skies were almost completely clear. The wind and sun dried the surface of the vast courtyard, where we had announced the meeting, to dust!

We went again to our knees, in gratitude to God.

Then at sundown, the clouds regathered. Indications were that, by meeting time, every unsheltered inch of the city would be drenched with water.

Yet the people came, many of them out of curiosity— having heard of Bob Findley's boldness in saying, "Tell everyone you can that God is going to roll back the clouds, and give us fair weather tonight."

When we entered the railway courtyard that evening, fully fifteen thousand people stood waiting to see and hear the message of the young man who dared to promise that, in the midst of the rainy season, his God could perform a miracle.

Bob Findley was not able to attend that night. After speaking in the morning, so exhausted he could scarcely fill the appointment, a nagging cold took over and closed his throat. There was nothing for him to do but rest.

When I left the room, though, he said, "I'll be in bed while you preach, but I want you to stand before those people and boast about our Lord's power to answer prayer."

It did not rain throughout the service that night. As Bob had suggested, I boasted about the power of our God and—as kindly as I could, reprimanded those who had not believed.

God gave us a mighty harvest that night! Among those who came to Christ was a dear old man, nearing his eightieth birthday, who became one of the spiritual stalwarts of our work during the concluding days.

CHAPTER NINETEEN

And the Rain Did Not Fall

Yes, the Lord God of Elijah was with us at Inchon.

The day following that first outdoor meeting, ominous clouds again blanketed the sky. Yet, by nightfall they were driven back, and it did not rain. This happened, without fail, on through the week.

Finally, the Inchon-area farmers began to worry.

"Look!" they reasoned among themselves. "These men prayed and God stopped the rain. Maybe the lack of rain will ruin our rice crop! We had better go and see the pastors, and see if they can't talk to these Americans and find out if this is going to spoil our harvest."

So they came to the pastors, who in turn came to Bob Findley and me for the answer.

By this time God had filled us with holy boldness. We felt as though we were living in the time of Acts, with a faith that could ask God for the impossible and believe in advance that it would be done.

"We can't let it rain until these meetings end," I said.

Then Bob Findley spoke up. God bless him for his faith and vision! "You tell the farmers this," he said. "We will pray that our God will keep the storm clouds back only until our meetings close on Sunday night. Tell them that then we will pray that God will let the rain come, and give them all the water they need."

"Bob," I half-whispered, "you know this would be sheer presumption under any other situation. Frankly, buddy, I wouldn't dare to talk as you have talked. But I believe you're right. In my own heart, I know that God is going to hold back the rain."

Turning to the pastors, I said. "We shall trust God to hold back the rain until the meetings end. But I have one request. I need Monday and Tuesday after the meetings to finish my photography." (I was taking footage for the film "28th Parallel," which we released shortly after returning to the States.) "May I pray that the rain will be held back until Wednesday?"

Soberly, as though we had a written contract before us, the pastors agreed, and left to convey their information to the worried farmers.

That night twenty thousand people came. And it did not rain. The campaign came to a conclusion, a glorious conclusion with multitudes hearing the Word and hundreds coming to a knowledge of Christ as Saviour.

And it did not rain.

Monday, Bob Findley and I gathered our things together and traveled the twenty-five miles to Seoul for some photography. Tuesday, also, we spent the day grinding out valuable footage. Tuesday night Bob got on a train bound for South Korea, to preach in a leprosarium.

Photography completed, I packed my bags preparatory to leavng next day for Japan.

Wednesday morning, when I rolled out of bed, threatening clouds filled the sky. At noon, as I journied to the airport, drops began to fall.

I checked in at customs and the ticket office, and boarded my plane. Moments later, the pilot taxied the big craft out onto the main runway. For a minute, he tested the motors.

Then we took off.

The pattern took us from Seoul's Kimpo airport out

across Inchon. Rain came down in sheets, making the ground scarcely visible. I could well imagine what the farmers were talking about!

In my heart, I thanked God for the showers of blessing which had come. What a great and mighty God! How foolish of me ever to question His will or doubt His might!

I prayed that I might have left some blessing in Korea. I thanked God for the blessing Korea had been to me.

CHAPTER TWENTY

A Return Visit To Korea

I wish that I might end my story with an account of the next few days.

Journeying on to Japan, God let me see more of His manifested power. I had wonderful fellowship with Dave Morken and his Youth for Christ leaders in Tokyo. I had a chance to see first-hand the work being done by the missionaries, by Inter-Varsity and Pocket Testament League and others.

It was also my privilege to visit Formosa, to attend church with Madame and Generalissimo Chiang Kai Shek. I believe firmly that the lands of the East have never seen leadership comparable to that of the Generalissimo. When future generations write the history of our muddled age, they will clearly vindicate this man who—like General Douglas MacArthur—fell target to the fiery darts of greed and the blunt-edged stabs of those with marred vision.

Much could be written about Japan and Formosa, wide open doors to the Gospel. If Christian Americans fail these strategic points today, then all Asia may be lost to the witness of Christ tomorrow.

But I cannot concern the conclusion of this account with further observations or evaluations of the greater Orient. I have not finished telling about Korea.

Before the year ended, I returned.

It was in bitter December. Communism had driven MacArthur's U.N. troops down into the narrow Pusan beachhead. But the great strategist kept a move ahead of them, and staged the brilliant landing at Inchon.

From there on, the caldron boiled uncertainly. U.N. troops drove north of the Parallel. Pyongyang, Red stronghold, fell. (How many sleepless nights I have spent longing to preach the Gospel in Pyongyang!)

Northward went the soldiers of freedom, pursuing the almost demoralized brigands of tyranny. G.I.'s from your town and mine dreamed of an early trip home. Some of them even sighted the Yalu.

You know the rest of the story, a story intricately confused in the unrest of international politics, a story written in the blood of young men.

I returned to Korea intent upon surveying the damage done to churches and other Christian centers, and to learn how the pastors and other spiritual workers had fared. With me, I took some eighteen thousand dollars donated by U.S. and Canadian Christians to alleviate the suffering of God's servants over there.

When I arrived in Seoul, I found it a bleeding, battered city. Red troops were only a few miles to the north, and thousands of refugees poured in grim panic across the Han, heading for whatever refuge they might find to the south.

With the tide having turned so unexpectedly, the city was a great hulk of confusion and indecision. I saw multitudes at work, trying to dig their way out of the terrible devastation, while, on the very streets where they worked, others fled in panic toward the Han, carrying or pulling on crude carts what few possessions they could take along.

From my hotel room in the heart of downtown Seoul, I got a close-up view of the city's ruin. The thing that struck me most, I believe, was that I could see many five and six story buildings which appeared undamaged. But then, scrutinizing them closer, I found that they were nothing more than burned-out shells. It appeared to me that at least sixty percent of the buildings were either bombed out or burned out.

That was before lethal fury again began pouring into the city.

People had already begun salvaging. Bricks were stacked in neat pyramids. All kinds of combustible material had been foraged by those who had the semblance of a stove in which to provide heat for cooking and warmth.

Refugees teemed everywhere. In droves they had poured out of the North, while U.N. forces yet protected the 38th Parallel. I saw whole families trudge down the streets, everyone from the father and mother to the little three-year-old children carrying loads on their backs. They, too, headed toward the Han—helpless, homeless, poverty-stricken, utterly bewildered.

I wept as I watched them, and my heart could not understand a world which will spend millions on destructive war but cannot show mercy to the innocent victims of international greed. There was nothing I could do. Absolutely nothing. The funds I had brought would be mere pittance, if used to help these mobs. I had to budget every penny carefully to do the job I felt had to be done for God's servants.

I marveled at these refugees, and made my way down to the Han to watch them cross. It was a frightening spectacle. The great bridge, which had so proudly handled the city's commerce, had been completely demolished except for its naked pylons standing gaunt against the dreary winter sky. In its place, a make-shift pontoon bridge spanned the river.

Plodding in a never-ending stream, the refugees made their way across. Ill-clad, their feet often wrapped in rags, it seemed less than human that they should set out in the bitter cold to tramp two are three hundred miles southward.

No destination, only flight—flight to nowhere.

Now and then a truck passed, so cumbered with people and belongings that it seemed impossible for them to make any headway.

"Yesterday," Roland Hill, Christian Church missionary, told me, "a truck charged two million yen to take a load of refugees from Seoul down to Pusan."

"How much money would that be in American dollars?" I asked.

"Eight or nine hundred dollars. That's a lot of money, when you consider that the average worker here makes only about fifty thousand yen a month—slightly over ten dollars."

I talked with Raymond Provost, a missionary whom I have come to love and deeply respect. He had just returned from driving sixty people, with all their belongings, toward the south.

He told me that on the return trip he had run into a stretch of road made precariously slippery by new-fallen snow. "I had to slow down considerably from our regular fast-driving speed of twenty miles an hour," he told me.

Leaving Taegu at about 6:30 A.M., it had taken awhile before he encountered the day's caravan of refugees. Then he came to a range of mountains.

"They have small railroad tunnels for northbound traffic to pass through," he said. "Traffic southbound uses the road, because that is by far the direction most people are traveling."

When army vehicles must convoy through, civilian transportation is forced to vacate the highway completely, and to try and find side trails over which to continue moving.

"Coming down, we had to go over the mountain

to make way for convoys," he continued. "It wasn't bad going, but coming back the snow had made the road very dangerous. For fifteen miles the road was one-way, hardly room anywhere for vehicles to meet or pass. We saw many trucks which had slid off the side, and had been abandoned because there was no way to get them back into operation.

"But the pitiful sights were the big trucks with refugees piled on them. When one of them toppled into the ditch, the people would stand around them completely bewildered. I met several where the people had built a fire to keep warm, while the driver stood sobbing like a baby because there was nothing he could do.

"We got out of the mountains about five o'clock, grateful to God that we had encountered no mishap. There were still six hours of driving back to Seoul, if the roads were good, but we decided to keep on.

"When we left Taejon, it was getting dark. Forty miles north of Taejon, we ran into a blizzard. Snow caked on the windshields so fast the wiper couldn't get it off fast enough. Bridges had been blown out all along the way, and we had to use the temporary passages. In normal driving, one could find these without difficulty. In a blizzard, it was a different story. Even though another truck had passed a quarter of a mile ahead of us, by the time we reached the stream his tracks had been completely obliterated by the snow. So we wasted a lot of time crossing creeks and small rivers.

"But the most pitiful thing I ever saw was when we went up a long hill at about seven o'clock. There was a village through which we passed, with houses close to the road on both sides. In between a few of the houses, the embankment was too steep for dwellings to be built.

"Trucks would slip first to one side and then to another, striking against the houses. If they slid into an open space, it was just too bad.

"I pulled my truck to a stop, because another truck was approaching. I turned out my lights, which was the signal for him to come on. He also turned out his lights, thus signaling for me to come. I blinked for two or three minutes, because I had found a suitable place for us to meet, but he refused to move. So I moved slowly forward, inching through the mess of trucks which had slid into houses and had been unable to get back onto the road.

"I came up to where this truck stood, stopping about a hundred feet in front of it, because it stood squarely in the middle of the road. I pulled off to the side as far as I could go, almost sliding into a house, and blinked my lights for the driver to proceed.

"At last he did. But he traveled no more than ten feet when his truck slid dizzily to the side. There was no house to stop him, and he careened over a twenty foot embankment.

"People jumped like scattering flies. But not all of them escaped the accident. Of the thirty refugees on the truck, ten were either killed or seriously wounded."

CHAPTER TWENTY - ONE

Deliverance

Because of the looming peril of new hostilities, I lost no time getting about my mission. I thanked God for what an American dollar could do for suffering Christians, thanked Him for those back home who cared enough to help supply the funds. Without the aid of Dr. Frank Phillips and Paul "First Mate Bob" Meyers, my co-workers in World Vision, Inc., and those who continued to give and pray, it would not have been possible for me to accomplish what I did, when a little meant so much.

I remember one orphanage, by way of example, where I had visited during my first journey through South Korea. It had remained in operation, because the Orientals loved children and the Red soldiers who passed by had decided not to molest the property or its occupants.

A godly Korean woman ran the orphanage, with the assistance of a half-dozen others, some of them registered nurses. Their supplies were gone, and hunger had begun to creep inside the walls of their humble compound.

The woman in charge had gone to each of her workers, and said, "War clouds are rolling over us again. Only God knows what the future holds. There is not rice enough for more than a few days. Unless God works a miracle . . ." She choked back a sob. It seemed utterly impossible that help could come, not in the midst of so much confusion. "Perhaps you had better leave me. There is time yet for you to flee southward."

Not a one of them left. "We will stay with you," they told her. "Forget about our salaries. And if there is not enough food, we will trust God with you. He knows all about us. He hasn't forgotten that we are here, trying to serve Him."

Trusting God, this woman made plans to keep her orphanage in operation. Somehow, funds would come, even though the prospect was utterly bleak.

Just before the last morsel of rice was cooked and served to the children, God led me to visit that orphanage. It had been on my heart, because I felt that—even in the midst of Communist re-occupation—this work would continue.

When I came to the compound, the woman in charge was completely dumbfounded. She did not know I had returned from America. When I gave her funds with which to continue through the winter, she fell to her knees before me as one in worship.

She wept, and I wept—begging her to get to her feet. For it was not I who had given the money, I told her. God had merely given me the privilege of being the channel through which the money was raised and brought to Korea.

"Give my deepest thanks to the Christians in America," she told me. "May God reward them!"

Time after time it was my privilege to assist the work of the Gospel in this manner. Each day that passed brought fresh impact to the conviction which had begun stirring in my heart back in America when first the suggestion was made that I should return.

My greatest concern was for the Christian workers —the seed of the Gospel in Korea. If the Communists succeeded in driving back into Seoul—which they soon did—then they would unquestionably inflict revenge moves against those who, like the Christians, were admittedly in favor of the United Nations.

Working with such missionary stalwarts as Bill Shaw, I was able to secure boxcars on a train heading south. We secured enough for the passage of six hundred Christian leaders, including women and children.

Of the eighteen boxcars on that train, loaded with refugees, nearly all of them were Christians. It was a thrilling sight.

I looked at their faces, tense with the mingled emotions of that moment. Some of them were the relatives of the forty-two Seoul-area clergymen and church leaders who had, so recently, been summoned for a "discussion" by the Communist leaders. They had not been heard from since, even when U.N. forces succeeding in penetrating almost to the Manchurian border.

They did not want to flee, if it meant to leave one anxious hungry heart unshepherded. But they realized the necessity of preserving spiritual leadership, so they were willing to go.

The air tingled with drama and spiritual emotion as the train finally creaked out of Seoul's bomb-riddled station. It would be a long journey, but they would lighten it with their songs and testimony and their unwavering confidence in the omnipotence of their God.

Only eternity can tabulate the value of that trainload!

CHAPTER TWENTY - TWO

Taegu and Farewell

My ministry in Korea began in the city of Taegu.

It was a different city when I returned, to fellowship again with Dr. Howard Moffatt, Arch Campbell and their co-workers. It moved me deeply to watch them minister to the throngs of refugees milling through and about the city, for Taegu was a hub in the flight out of Seoul.

The presbytery of the Taegu area was in session when I came there, and they extended to me the privilege of addressing them briefly. Some fifty or sixty pastors attended, and I heard them tell their pathetic stories of ruined churches and martyred Christians.

That evening, when we returned to the Campbell home, three young men awaited us on the veranda. Their feet were bound with cloth shoes. Two of them wore overcoats, but had no shirts. The third wore a woman's topcoat.

Arch Campbell recognized them. They had come from his former parish at Sun Chon in North Korea. Hitch-hiking and on foot they had traveled several hundred miles.

They brought tragic news.

The entire group of pastors in their city, over twenty in number, had been massacred by the furiously angry Communists. The shock of this terrible thing was still on the faces of these young men.

This was only the beginning of startling news which I was to hear. I learned of one city where hundreds of people were brutally slain, because the Reds found Bibles or hymn books in their homes. Pastors and their families were tortured, churches sacked, Christians driven from their holdings.

I think that most indelible on my memory, however, is a morning prayer meeting I attended there in Taegu, shortly before returning to America. It was one of those pre-dawn gatherings, and when we reached the church where it was held, fully three thousand had already come.

I tried to bring them a message, but it was short— probably one of the shortest I have ever given. For what could I say to those who knew so much more than I did about faith and patience and dependence upon the Bible for spiritual sustenance?

My words came with extreme labor, as I looked out at the people, for I knew how fresh were the pains of horror and loss in many of their hearts. I could look forward to a trip back to America, back to so much that is so thoughtlessly taken for granted. They had a future as black as despair itself.

Yet there was no despair in that prayer meeting.

They prayed for their suffering brethren, asking God to give them courage and, above all else, an unwavering witness regardless of circumstances. They prayed for the salvation of their enemies. They prayed that soon the Gospel might have free course in the land.

Tears flowed down my cheeks as I listened. I had brought along a tape recorder, and to this day I am moved when I listen to the voices of those people that morning. In solemn concert, as was their custom, they cried out to God.

Then, suddenly, someone began a song. First a few voices, more, and then the entire congregation. The song they sang reveals, more than anything I might say further, the character of Korean Christians.

For in the stillness of that morning hour, in the anticipation of imminent death and destruction, they sang:

> Come, Thou Fount of every blessing,
> Tune my heart to sing Thy grace;
> Streams of mercy, never ceasing,
> Call for songs of loudest praise.
> Teach me some melodious sonnet,
> Sung by flaming tongues above;
> Praise the mount—I'm fixed upon it—
> Mount of Thy redeeming love.

Printed in the United States of America